You!

Make Organizational Change Successful

Tim Moon

Dedication

This book is dedicated to my wife and son, who made it possible for me to have a successful professional career. Their support over the years enabled me to navigate the stepping stones of success, which, with each step, brought more responsibility and bigger challenges. They were at my side to encourage me through the hard times any professional career puts before you.

Everything from watching my son grow to fishing trips to vacations to simple soup and sandwich lunches made a huge difference in my life. To this, I owe a debt of gratitude to my wife and son for being the best at helping me along. Thank you, I love you both.

Acknowledgment

Without the Lord by my side, this journey would be more challenging than it was. His wisdom and love guide me.

I would like to acknowledge all the professionals I've had the privilege to work with over the years. Fortunately, I worked with some of the best leaders, managers, friends, and mentors a person could ask for. They allowed me to have a dream career. Without their influence on my life, this book would not have been possible.

To my parents, siblings, relatives, and extended family, I thank you for keeping me grounded in my roots. This kept my head straight and manifested the best traits and values a person can have.

Preface

Change in an organization is one of the most complex processes to lead, manage, implement, and sustain. Unless you are in one of the very few organizations with people who have a specific skill set to lead a change effort or train leadership on the tenets of change, you are pretty much on your own.

Most people who have a post-high school education, whether it is a certification, associate degree, or doctorate, took a class (to some degree) with change discussion or textbook examples. If you don't have any formal education, many working individuals have exposure to change from an employee perspective to some level. So, it should not be a surprise to anyone that change will be part of their work life at various points in their professional career.

This book hopes to enlighten people in the workforce about their role in an organizational change process. This applies to the most junior employees, senior management, and the highest levels of leadership in the organization. Additionally, this book can help small business owners, non-government organizations, and non-profit organizations employ an aggressive approach to change with an equally strong follow-through that embeds change into the organization. In all cases, this book will prove its worth beyond expectations.

About the Author

Tim Moon is a Midwesterner who sought adventure and opportunity after graduating high school. A twenty-eight-year career in the US Navy saw Tim reach the top levels of the enlisted force, with his last ten years working at the executive level of various organizations. Tim continued working with the federal government in various capacities and quickly reached executive-level positions as a civil servant.

While on active duty, Tim earned his bachelor's degree and then, after retiring, earned his master's degree in international business studies. With a desire to give back, he began to teach part-time as an adjunct professor at two colleges. He taught business courses at the graduate level and emergency management courses at the college level.

Always looking for a new adventure, Tim sought job positions over job locations. This took him and his family to locations throughout the United States and at numerous locations in the Asia-Pacific region.

The journey continues, but instead of moving around, Tim and his wife now travel around the United States to see the beauty of this country and travel to international locations to enjoy the beauty of this world.

Contents

Chapter 1: Motivation for Change!

What drives us to embrace change? Is it the promise of a brighter future, the fear of stagnation, or perhaps a combination of both? In the ever-changing landscape of business, the ability to adapt and evolve is not just advantageous—it's imperative. But what fuels this willingness to change? How can we harness the power of motivation to propel ourselves and our organizations forward?

You can look at change through a multitude of lenses, but it is important to understand that motivation will pave the way to success much easier, faster, and with better results. Every person in the world, let alone your organization, is motivated differently, making it almost impossible to define a one-size-fits-all strategy to inspire change. However, as leaders in an organization, you are challenged to know your people well enough to utilize motivation strategies that will produce the greatest impact on the workforce.

Remember – it's not the change, it's the people!

That's right, you change the organization. When you see a change plan, you can read it on a piece of paper, think through the proposed change, and understand it as best you can. You can speak to people within your organization to better understand what the change is all about. When you do speak to others, seek only the facts because, without fail, you'll get all the opinions you don't need.

These conversations will get you closer to understanding what the organization would like to do or has already decided to do. At this point, however, it's just a plan on a piece of paper. The actual execution and implementation of change happen when you and everyone in the organization get involved. Isn't that a powerful thought? Yes, you, the person sitting behind your desk eight hours a day processing paperwork, writing reports, becoming the best PowerPoint slide maker, or (app-ing, as in using applications on your phone or computer) you're behind off.

That's right, you are the person who makes change successful. Who do you see sitting at the desk next to you, behind you, or in the office across the hall? Do you see motivation as well? Whether or not you are intimately involved with whatever the organization has decided to do, each person in the organization plays an important role when it comes to change within the organization.

That's pretty cool, empowerment at its best. Think of your role and decide what you can do to be the person who not only believes in what your organization is doing but is motivated to be part of the solution to improve the organization.

You must be a player. Imagine walking up to the water cooler and overhearing a conversation that is counterproductive to where the organization wants to go. Do you engage in the conversation, or do you just walk away? Engaging the conversation is the first step in becoming a major player within the organization. Chances are your workmates either don't understand the intent of the change or disagree with it, making them part of the challenge to implement change successfully. Think of yourself as a change policeman. Your role is to blow the whistle and correct the deficiency or deficient thought processes of those who are not on board with the pending change in the organization.

A word of caution here: that person you're listening to could be a supervisor or someone in a leadership position who influences the organization. This doesn't mean you should not say anything; actually, the opposite is the case. When a senior person hears a junior person provide input on any topic, including pending change, you influence the process.

So again, it goes back to people, back to you, not the change itself that needs correcting or adjusting. We will delve into it later in Chapter 5 of the book- "Train of Change."

Influence Your Workmates by Educating Them on The Purpose of Change

You change people along with policies or procedures. Changing people may be the most challenging effort within your organization. Employees and organizational leaders must adapt to and understand the need for change. A goal of having a large percentage of people implementing change will find a higher rate of success. This happens when the workforce puts forth the effort to bring the organization's employees and stakeholders on board with the change effort as quickly as possible.

The question remains—how do you excite your employees and your workforce? You may be the representative for your department, division, or code by attending change meetings, making it incumbent upon you to motivate those you represent.

Policy drives planning, design, or end state. Think of something as simple as the use of a new form. Internally, the need for that change will not succeed or make a true difference unless the workforce adopts the change. How can managers ensure employees and subordinates believe in and commit to the change?

No matter how large or small the change is, similar principles apply.

Hey, leader, you're not right all the time. Using your positional power to guide a change process will ensure the process is complete as designed. But once your focus goes somewhere else or your priorities change (many times for a valid reason), your effort of leading the change process will probably alter, probably reduce significantly, and allow your team or subordinates to shift their priorities as well. You must keep your team and subordinates engaged in the process, stick to the plan, and make yourself replaceable.

'What, me replaceable?' you think.

Yup, you. Think of the benefits of having more than one person equally adept in the change you or your company want or need to implement. Think of load sharing, flexibility, and the ability to enact parallel efforts of the plan. Think of the number of people who are committed to the successful implementation of change because you motivated them to strive for success.

If you are one of those leaders who believe the success or failure of the company rests solely on your shoulders and do not trust anyone below you, then you provide a barrier to motivation. Not to mention, you should prepare for many long days in the office because you'll need extra time to get all your work done.

So, what is the motivation for change all about?

It's all about the look, the nod, the wink, the expression, the aura of people. You can tell when a supervisor, peer, co-worker, or subordinate likes what they are doing. You can tell when they are excited about an issue or event. You can tell just by observing them that they are all in for the ride this particular change will bring. Of many reasons why people are motivated, a couple are more evident than others.

Some are all in because of a personal or professional agenda or maybe because they see the benefit this change effort will make to their department or the organization as a whole. Some are all in because they dislike how old processes work. Additionally, you can become motivated by others about the impending change when you sense a feeling of belonging or being part of something important, something better, or bigger than yourself. While others can be responsible for understanding the big picture or larger goal in a way that impacts you or your team, you see motivation levels shift more towards the stated goal.

You witness intangible motivators become tangible motivators that include feeling a sense of teamwork, being part of the team, and being a contributor.

These tangible motivators are evident every time you participate in the change effort, whether you are leading the entire change effort or contributing to the level your expertise requires.

Knowing your motivation began sometime earlier, it's pretty neat when it's all said and done after the change project, including implementation, is complete—you will feel good! You can enjoy that good feeling of accomplishment and that of contributing to the improvement made for your organization. You'll see the sustainment of the change you worked so hard to implement.

You will witness a transition as you become a strong advocate for the new policy, you have a stronger commitment to your company's customers, and, equally important, you'll be a subject matter expert to new employees who join the organization after implementation. Remember, it all starts with motivation.

I Feel The Power!

Can you feel it when your workforce is excited about a forthcoming change?

You will see people talking about how this change will impact their area of expertise, even if the change is small or may not be that relevant at all. Remember, 'excitement' has two meanings: happy and not happy! Excitement turns to anxiety for those in the not-happy camp. People who feel positive energy from the impending change seem to automatically agree with or feel comfortable with the process and end state.

Seeing the excitement in the workforce is a great feeling as a leader. When employees come to you with ideas to make a process better, easier, or more efficient, you know the workforce is energized.

You get to this level of excitement when, as a leader, you use your strongest communication skills to ensure the workforce understands the macro-level version of the change and micro-detailed information that makes the difference at each level of the organization.

Simply stating the new process will streamline your efforts only scratches the surface of what you have to communicate. Using the earlier example, processing forms is good for the macro statement. However, adding micro data points to explain why the change has benefits is a must.

This includes automatically entering basic information such as name, date, and department and selecting relevant options from drop-down menus or checkboxes, significantly reducing the time and effort required to complete the form.

However, when the workforce that executes the change daily understands, for instance, that a cumbersome form that used to take twenty keystrokes to complete will now take eight keystrokes to complete, it will have great meaning and increase buy-in for the change.

Of course, we can't forget the training required for each employee to fully understand how the new system works. So where does this take us? For your workforce, it is possible that an inner feeling, or your inner culture, of knowing the end state and knowing their place in enabling change is enough.

You will know they are motivated when you hear the excitement in their voice. When they speak, they speak as the owner of the change, and you can sense in their voice the importance of implementing this change.

Why Change?

Change is required in an ever-changing, dynamic world where competition fuels the fire of every organization to be the best at providing the best customer service, product, or service. In a global market, you compete not only within your host country but also with every company worldwide that does the same thing you do.

If you own a small business, such as a bakery, you compete with every bakery within a defined area of your business. Even a company that makes the tastiest donuts due to their secret recipe still competes for customers. Technology is one example of how organizations and businesses must change to stay competitive. You could probably think of a handful or more of the reasons why your company or small business has to make changes to remain competitive. It becomes a question of survivability for any business to do so.

Personalities are involved, and I think we all can agree that one of the major components of successful change is buy-in. So, let's look at buy-in and consider how important this can be to your organization.

I remember one evening walking in the park and seeing a youth soccer game between kids about the age of five or six. I stopped to watch the game and saw this young person kick the soccer ball into the goal.

This was after many minutes of the ball going nowhere because these kids were just learning how to play soccer. But when that ball went into the goal, I knew immediately who the father of that young player was.

I knew from the incredibly exciting response he displayed—jumping, screaming, laughing, praising his child for making what turned out to be the only score of that game.

As I watched this father act as if he had just won a huge lottery, I wondered, "What caused this reaction?" My immediate answer was that this guy had total buy-in to his child and the youth soccer program.

His buy-in was so strong; at least at this point, you could have asked him to bring post-game snacks for the rest of the season, and he would have done it. That's strong buy-in.

So, from here, we have to ask: how do we generate a commensurate amount of enthusiasm within the workforce and organization? You might say it's apples and oranges; you can't compare enthusiasm for your child's activities and your work environment. I think you can.

If you are early on in your professional career, or even mid-career, and you wrote down what's important to you, your family and work would be at the top of the list, at least in the top five.

So, let's agree that a person can have an equal amount of passion for their work as they do for other priorities in their life, and we simply look at or display that passion differently.

Let's discuss the mental and psychological aspects of getting excited about change. Why does our brain light up when something cool happens? And how do we get pumped enough to do something about it? Think about the dad cheering for his child's soccer goal.

Why does he go wild? It's not just because his kid kicked a ball into a net. It's deeper than that. First, there's a strong emotional connection. He's invested in his child's success, so their achievement feels like his own.

Then there's the feeling of validation. Seeing his child score isn't just a goal—it's proof that they're growing, learning, and succeeding. That hits home for any parent. Plus, excitement is contagious.

When we see someone else hyped up, our brains mirror that feeling. So, when the dad starts jumping around, other people join in, too.

How can we channel this energy into organizational change? It's about giving people a reason to care. When employees understand why the change matters and how they fit into the bigger picture, they are likelier to get on board.

Clear communication and support are key, too. Nobody likes feeling lost or left out, so providing guidance and resources can ease the transition.

However, excitement is temporary, according to Neil Patel's article *"The Psychology of Excitement: How to Better Engage Your Audience,"* he talks about excitement lasting for around twenty minutes based on the type of excitement he discusses. Now, think about being in a room with your peers or supervisors for twenty minutes. You can use this temporary excitement to influence others during this heightened emotional state.

How do you react when someone in the meeting is excited about the topic being discussed? You might feel a bit of adrenaline.

If not, you may think to yourself, "What's this all about?" Just asking the question is a signal of wanting to buy in.

Going back to soccer dad, the excitement he displayed when his child scored a goal was infectious.

I found myself getting excited for him—I wanted some of the joy he was feeling because it looked so good on him. The other parents were equally happy with the goal because they knew the team was winning, so the transfer of excitement and emotion was quick and effective. Soccer dad was the lead, but the team knew it was beneficial to them in the long run, in the game.

That's powerful!

If the leader starts off the meeting with negativity, despair, or an attitude of no value to what you are doing, the rest of the team sees that and feels it. They may see it as approval to disregard any future mention of this topic or allow them to push back on any ideas associated with that topic. Conversely, if you're the person who benefits from the change, it's easy to be the excited person in the room. You know your environment, so make statements accordingly to impact and influence the team.

How do you change organizational culture to achieve organizational change, and how do you ensure "automatic" buy-in? Good leaders understand that a strong organizational culture will make a significant difference in the amount and level of buy-in from employees. However, before that leader attempts to get buy-in from their workforce, they should take to heart John Maxwell's answer to the question he routinely gets: "Do you think my people will buy into my vision?"

He answers, "First, tell me this. Do your people buy into you?" And you say?

Let's talk about John Maxwell's viewpoint. He emphasizes the importance of culture in achieving organizational change. He suggests that a great culture starts with a vision or mission statement, instilling purpose and inspiring authentic work. However, vision alone is not enough; it must be connected to the actual values of the company. Maxwell also stresses the importance of behavior, symbols, and systems as outward displays of what is valued, which points to culture.

Culture is created as a result of the messages employees receive about how to behave in the organization. To ensure "automatic" buy-in, Maxwell suggests that companies must either start with the right people who share the company values or hire people willing to embrace them. Additionally, companies must create a winning culture to support their vision, and this culture must be supported by guidelines for the winning behaviors and mindsets necessary to achieve the goals. Finally, Maxwell advises leaders to take stock of the company's physical surroundings, embrace its history, and leverage the element of narrative to build a cohesive culture.[1]

Meanwhile, Matt Palmquist said, "Emotions can get in the way of rational decision-making. Anger, in particular, can make employees increase their commitment to a failing plan." This is almost a drop-the-mic statement. Even if you like the plan, you may not want to participate—there's just too much going on and no time in your already busy schedule to mess around with this change. So, a manager who approaches change without the willingness to use every tool in the motivation toolbox gives you an easy out.

You just listen to your manager and think, *'If they don't like it, why should I?'* Although you have this thought or feeling, you

---

[1]https://johnmaxwellleadershippodcast.com/episodes/john-maxwell-three-components-of-cultivating-culture

must walk away from it and take on a positive attitude about any process that improves the organization.

Your attitude and behavior can shape the success of those big changes happening in your organization. Let's learn how you can tap into your motivation to drive some serious positive change within your team or company!

Chapter 2: Individual Dynamics

Ever found yourself lost in the winding roads of change? It's a challenge we've all faced, especially when our professional journey takes unexpected turns.

How do we navigate this complex terrain within ourselves? What strategies can we employ to stay grounded amidst the whirlwind of transitions? When uncertainty looms large, how do we tap into our inner resilience? And let's not underestimate the importance of self-awareness—how does tuning our thoughts and feelings guide us through the turbulence?

In the process of change, individual factors are crucial in shaping the outcome. Each person brings unique perspectives, experiences, and attitudes to the table, which can greatly influence how they perceive and respond to change.

From their level of buy-in and enthusiasm to their willingness to adapt and embrace new ways of doing things, individual factors can either propel change forward or act as stumbling blocks.

Notably, the psychological aspect of change—the journey from thought to action—plays a pivotal role in our ability to adapt and thrive amidst organizational transformations.

Thought to action is hard. Have you ever said, "I was going to read that email attachment before the meeting but just did not get to it!"

You know the plan. You've seen the implementation strategy and timeline. You think about it every day walking to your work area. Now what? For every action, there's a reaction, so what will you do today to move the change process forward?

You're probably thinking, "I've got forty hours of work in my inbox as it is."

Additionally, you'll need to allocate time for the necessary meetings this week, where you're expected to attend and provide updates on the specific tasks assigned to you or your team in the change plan.

Indeed, that requirement is yours this week and every week for the next few weeks. This seems like a great time to pull out those time management processes that always seem to make a lot of sense.

Time management is critical, as are topics and processes discussed throughout the book. For now, let's simply put thought into action. You know what works best or what offers the best option for you, the department, and the organization, so step up and do it.

You are known as Mister Know-It-All (I know, just ask me), and this is the best time to convince others you really know your profession, your place in the organization, and that you're valuable to this process.

Yup, Mr. Know-It-All, the person you think you are now front and center, just where you want to be. Take it in, accept it, capitalize on it, and make those thoughts some of the most productive actions you've taken, maybe since you began working at the organization.

It should feel good, kind of like stretching out when you haven't exercised in a while; it feels that good. You know, it hurts a little because you're not used to that soreness feeling, but it will get better with time.

So, there you go, smart, humble, confident, and productive person. Be the asset to this movement you are capable of and show your worth. Ouch! I just pulled a muscle at the first meeting. That's okay because, more than likely, your thoughts were good; you just missed some pieces of the puzzle that would have rocked their world. Don't give up; keep the thoughts coming; the working group appreciates it, and as will be discussed very soon, your inner culture will drive success during this and many more meetings (that interrupt your weekly routine) and place you just a little bit further behind in getting to the next item on your to-do list.

Let's delve into the motivation for buy-in and follow-through from an individual dynamic perspective. We'll explore buy-in to change multiple times in this book, and it's crucial to prioritize this aspect of change if you want any chance of successful implementation within the organization. But for now, let's focus on your motivation for change, which drives buy-in and ultimately provides much-needed follow-through.

Motivation, as defined by Webster's Dictionary, is "a motivating force, stimulus, or influence." The individual dynamics type of motivation we're discussing here isn't much different, except that with some proposals or plans for change, you may find it challenging to motivate yourself, let alone those you are responsible for or associate with.

So, if needed, at least start with showing interest! I mean, come on, you probably do it with many other issues you deal with in your line of work, and you have success, so why not here? When looking at motivation in a positive light, your motivation equals or defines the buy-in we need.

Looking ahead (and in the case of some change processes, it could amount to months and months of hard work), your organization gets to the point where the change plan is reaching some of the last steps.

Individual dynamics could also apply to your portion of a larger plan, and the follow-through, or follow-up process, becomes more important than you imagined. Just when you think it's finally here—no more meetings, progress reports, or Change X project issues on your to-do list. What now? Well, the next change project you're involved with may support the one you just completed, which, in turn, supports the larger plan. How do you approach your recent success?

Jump for joy, have a party, ask for time off or a bonus, or put it all behind you? All have merit, but let's stay on course and not steer away from what's important—follow through after the implementation phase so your effort to this point will not go to waste.

Loop back to the initial spark that ignited your motivational fire, that fire getting you to where you are now and the fuel that keeps your fire burning.

However, in this case, you only need to be concerned with the huge responsibility of the follow-through phase that ensures your hard work pays off. In other words, take a return-on-investment type approach. Don't let yourself, your peers, or your organization slip away from the benefits this change brings to the organization.

"Yeah, but that's hard, and I've got new projects I need to focus on."

You just didn't say that, did you? Let me first tell you that you are correct; you do have new projects, and it seems a normal thing to do—moving on to your next great adventure, that is.

However, this will be the worst decision you will make regarding the just-completed specific change process, letting all that hard work go down the drain without care.

"But they got it. They know what to do."

Really? How do you know? Let's cut to the chase by recognizing that a strong plan ensuring the change project becomes part of your organizational culture takes time—sometimes months or years—before you see the new processes become a daily norm. Embrace that, and don't deny it; make it part of your long-term plan. You may only need to conduct periodic checks or see it in the people who carry out the day-to-day operations. However, without fail, you must have a plan to follow through with the change once it is fully implemented to ensure you can claim success for all your hard work.

Your dynamics have the potential to derail progress or derail your mental stamina with tangential conversations. I use the phrase tangential conversation to describe someone when you ask one thing, and the response is nowhere near the topic. Before moving on, let's uncover what professionals have to say about a tangential conversation.

Dennis C. Tanner, in his book *"Forensic Aspects of Communication Sciences and Disorders,"* defines "Tangential speech" as "A communication disorder in which the train of thought of the speaker wanders and shows a lack of focus, never returning to the initial topic of the conversation."

This is where we'll take this portion of the chapter. Your ability to stay focused on the topic at hand is critical for planting yourself on the side of influence and subject matter expertise. There is also a term called 'tangentially,' which, as described by the website GoodTherapy.org, "is the tendency to speak about topics unrelated to the main topic of discussion. While most people engage in tangentially from time to time, constant and extreme tangentially may indicate an underlying mental health condition, particularly schizophrenia."

We don't need to take this topic so far that it leaves an impression that everyone you associate with has schizophrenia, but sometimes, with some people, you kind of get that feeling! As I stated earlier, my definition of a tangential conversation is when you ask a specific question, and the response you get is not even close to the question asked. I think you can relate to this definition, and you probably have a person in mind right now.

The impact tangential conversations can have on your ability to maintain focus on yourself and possibly the change team is significant. Having someone involved in the change process who avoids a direct conversation, or a direct question does not 'move the ball forward.' It can cause a divide in your effort. Team members who still do not have complete buy-in to the change at hand may find refuge in tangential conversations to help them find a good reason the change process should not continue or show their lack of interest in the change project.

As weak as this may sound, tangential conversations are a reality the change agent should be aware of. Unfortunately, the other person(s) just wants to talk about what's on their mind. This seems popular with politicians but frustrating with friends, family, co-workers, peers, seniors, and subordinates.

What was the question again?

Your philosophy and approach to work, or your inner culture, are traits that support your success as a leader and your ability to influence others. Your inner culture is an essential element of any solution. You're familiar with organizational culture, or at least the term.

The context of organizational culture is familiar across all spectrums of leadership as it applies to organizations big and small.

Sometimes, you can pick up on an organization's culture very quickly because of some obvious signs like politeness, professional attitude, interaction between workers and others, etc.

However, with inner culture, the focus is on you. It demonstrates what drives your professional success or contributions to the organization. Some could refer to inner culture as interpersonal relationship traits, ego, or moral compass. Think of your inner culture as what makes you part of the solution or maybe even part of the problem.

Let's take a look at your norm. This is a self-assessment. Write on a piece of paper how you feel every day about work—satisfied, happy, content, excited, obligated, no energy, no spark, no desire.

I've had jobs where I was eager to get to work in the morning and felt bad about going home at the end of the day. I wasn't a workaholic but committed to the organization and very satisfied with my work environment; I felt on top of the world.

If you are excited and feel good about your business, job, or going to work, understanding your inner culture is for you. Now, think of things that change that feeling.

On the same piece of paper, write what bugs you and takes you out of your positive inner culture—an unruly customer, unpleasant client, tardiness, being cut off or not listened to, missed appointments, or deadlines. Just write down one.

Are you familiar with the time swindler?

You know, the person who stands at your desk or calls you and talks for 30 minutes about nothing mainly because they don't want to work, or they have nothing better to do. The time swindler has a negative inner culture; everything positive noted above isn't this person.

They are probably good people and contribute to the organization but don't possess the attributes for a positive inner culture.

If you are not excited about your business, job, or going to work, there is not much that would change you to like your job or what you're doing for the better unless you want it.

Your options boil down to either finding your sweet spot that re-establishes your inner culture or finding a new job. In both cases, if your inner culture is not one of success, passion, desire, or team membership, you must adjust to get there. Don't fake it. You must be willing to go all in for the organization in the context of your inner culture.

You wrote down a trait that describes your norm, your inner culture, and what you feel good about in your job. You also wrote down actions that take a toll on your positive daily norm. Is that negative trait or action something you can manage, or can it put you in a different mental state? Severely impact your inner culture? This self-examination can help you identify actions that you can be aware of and prepare yourself to ensure your norm of positivity always outweighs the negative forces you deal with on the job (and in life).

Now, let's define "all in": it's having enough commitment to the organization to be part of the solution. Sole proprietorships or small businesses of just a few people go all in every day as a matter of survivability. However, a consistent inner culture will allow for longer sustainability because there is less stress with being you. A steady course is the key to success. Don't allow others to influence the inner culture that makes you successful. Just say no to those influences. Know your role in the organization, meeting, gathering, on the phone, or interacting with clients.

Inducted into the Basketball Hall of Fame, Kareem Abdul-Jabbar sums it up perfectly with his quote:

"One man can be a crucial ingredient on a team, but one man cannot make a team."

What could be a distractor to this? Look for traits of others that may indicate their inner culture. Think of a meeting where you say to yourself, "That person doesn't want to be here." Comments, actions, or body language can flash a neon sign over that person. Bad day? Maybe. Who knows spring butt? That disruptive person who always has to ask a question or interrupt to make a comment for whatever reason they feel is necessary to jump in and make themselves heard.

This is an individual dynamic indicator of their inner culture, one of insecurity or a need to be recognized, accepted, or acknowledged. All are counter to what the team or organization needs to move forward.

Remember, your inner culture contributes to your professional success and the success of the organization.

Resolve

If you ask yourself, "What's my resolve to change culture, policy, structure?" how would you honestly answer it? If you answer in the positive, then, well, it's now a mission by golly. It's a mission because you have the change bug, and it's infectious, at least in you. Resolve is a trait strong enough to get you through even the hardest times in the change process. A dictionary definition of 'resolve,' according to Merriam-Webster, is "to reach a firm decision about."[2]

Resolve becomes an individual dynamic player when you decide to support or not, and the level of effort you need to be an impactful person to see the pending change succeed.

So, where does 'resolve' stack up on your list of traits? Once you think about it, it is probably pretty high on the list, but that's only when you think about resolve as an element of success.

Okay, I got it. I need the resolve to ensure a change process is successful. Yes, that and more. Just like with motivation, resolve must be a constant in the change process; otherwise, like a crack in a foundation, other traits can weaken you to a point where you have little to no focus (or at least the right focus) on the task at hand, which is the change.

Remember, total support for any change is incredible until you're tasked with writing an in-depth progress report. The extra effort required to complete these tasks can wreak havoc on your already full schedule, but your resolve will contribute to a great report.

---

[2] https://www.merriam-webster.com/dictionary/resolve

Very few companies include the word "resolve" in their mission statement. Mission statements typically consist of one or two powerful sentences that capture the purpose and perhaps the values of the company. Occasionally, you may come across a mission statement with four or five sentences that touch on their resolve to provide outstanding customer service or other mission traits. Don't let that influence you from keeping resolve in your bag of positive traits that contribute to individual dynamics.

Winston S. Churchill has a great quote:

"It is not enough that we do our best; sometimes, we must do what is required."

As we come to the end of this chapter, it's pretty evident that our individual dynamics drive us and indicate how determined we are. They're like a compass guiding us through the twists and turns of change, whether within ourselves or in our workplaces.

Getting a grip on these factors isn't just helpful; it's downright crucial for making headway in today's dynamic professional scene. Guess what's up next? We're diving into the interesting world of organizational dynamics, where we'll peel back the layers to see how these very principles shape the big picture in our workplace. You will identify traits in organizational dynamics that are separate but run parallel with individual dynamics.

Chapter 3: Organizational Dynamics

Now, let us comprehend the complex world of organizational dynamics by laying bare the underlying factors contributing to an organization's ability to implement change effectively.

By understanding organizational dynamics, we will gain insights into the visible and subtle aspects that shape the culture and functioning of a company.

By identifying several indicators of strong organizational dynamics and recognizing their implications, we will uncover how these dynamics can foster cohesion or create fragmentation within an organization.

Often referred to in terms of diversity, 'organizational dynamics' defines the ability of an organization to implement change effectively.

This means an organization has room in an eight-hour workday for a bit of banter, cheerful discussion, or playful competition. Or the opposite, a head down working at your desk atmosphere with limited breaks and short lunchtime where most people eat at their desks.

These dynamics are typically visible or understood by personnel within the company. Strong organizational dynamics can be easily recognized by visitors or those working with the company. Indicators of organizational dynamics that demonstrate a fragmented organization include work centers that are not in tune with each other, pockets of workers forming cliques, or comments from the workforce indicating they are unique or better than others in the organization.

It's important to note that organizational dynamics should not be confused with organizational culture traits mentioned in the previous chapter, as dynamics can be more negative but still have significant advantages.

To begin with, organizational dynamics are crucial for several reasons. They tend to be more pronounced in larger organizations due to the increased opportunity to leverage a diverse workforce. Take the field of information technology, for example. Within this domain, you'll find a variety of expertise, including skilled programmers, network engineers, network security managers, and developers, just to name a few. When these subject matter experts come together, they form a powerful team capable of implementing impactful changes in technology for the betterment of the company.

Moreover, organizational dynamics facilitate understanding for non-IT workers, enabling them to grasp how programs work within the company. This positive change ultimately benefits customers, who are the primary focus for companies. Even for smaller organizations, the same principle holds, albeit on a smaller scale. Every individual's contribution matters, regardless of project size. Whether it's one person or ten, the level of effort remains the same. Conversely, if a small organization has only one subject matter expert, their performance significantly impacts the implementation of change.

This holds true whether there's one expert or one hundred, depending on the scale of the change and the organization's size. While larger organizations may have a larger pool of talent to choose from, the fundamental premise remains unchanged. Hint: don't send a programmer when the plan calls for network security work.

So, let's circle back to the primary reason why organizational dynamics are crucial. The change affects everyone in the organization differently. Therefore, it falls on supervisors and leaders to understand their team members well enough to gauge their level of, or potential level of, commitment to the change initiative. While this task is not always easy, it often comes down to relying on simple instincts—doing whatever it takes to assess the commitment of peers, employees, and subordinates. Think inner culture.

In a large organization, a supervisor may undertake the task of selecting two individuals out of ten within their section or department for a change project. Initially, identifying these two candidates might seem relatively straightforward, as it could be based on their immediate reactions to the announcement of the change effort.

However, the scenario differs significantly in smaller organizations. Here, the task becomes more challenging as there may be only three individuals, or possibly just two, tasked with implementing change. In such cases, the selection process necessitates a deeper assessment of each person's skills, adaptability, and commitment to ensure the success of the change initiative.

Furthermore, organizational dynamics play a crucial role in supporting your company's mission and vision statements. It's rare to find an organization with a mission statement or vision that explicitly prioritizes getting things right the second time or tolerates delayed implementations, upgrades, or improvements. Quite the contrary, most mission statements emphasize efficiency, effectiveness, and cost savings as drivers of success and profitability.

Rather than embracing a philosophy of accepting delays or imperfections, companies typically strive for expedient results to bolster their bottom line. They prioritize attributes like efficiency, innovation, and adaptability in their corporate visions to foster motivation and drive success within the organization.

Negative traits of organizational dynamics mentioned earlier, such as delays or a reluctance to strive for perfection, can serve as positive motivators if the organization truly embodies its stated values. Imagine looking around the office and witnessing colleagues embracing a positive approach to every aspect of their work—tackling projects, implementing change efforts, or fostering collaboration. When organization dynamics open the door to such positivity, the entire workplace culture can transform.

Consider the ripple effect: when employees observe leadership actively promoting a positive outlook and embracing flexibility in the face of challenges, they're more likely to follow suit. Suddenly, setbacks become growth opportunities, and individuals feel empowered to contribute their best efforts without fear of reprimand for occasional missteps.

Moreover, a workplace culture that values positivity and adaptability can attract and retain top talent. Employees are more likely to feel satisfied and engaged when they perceive their organization as supportive and forward-thinking. This, in turn, enhances productivity, fosters innovation, and ultimately contributes to the organization's long-term success.

You can influence organizational dynamics in both directions. Positive, excitable actions—think of soccer dad in Chapter 1—are infectious with peers (leaders like it, too). Talking genuinely with peers in the department with the lion's share of responsibility for the change actions will cycle up, over, and back down through the organization.

It works like this: Rose in Operations talks to Jay in IT about how beneficial the new software changes will be for Operations once the changes are implemented. Jay, who is on the change team because of his IT expertise, is not excited about the change but still comments to his supervisor about Rose's interest in the change.

At a staff meeting, the IT supervisor makes a positive statement about their awareness of other departments' excitement about the pending change. Not only does the Operations supervisor acknowledge the statement, but all other department supervisors also hear this and think this must be great for the organization.

Since supervisors rarely quote statements from meetings and typically paraphrase, they will communicate to their subordinates the significant benefits of the ongoing software change in the IT department. And there you have it: you influenced organizational dynamics!

Remember, stakeholders play a pivotal role in guiding the trajectory of development initiatives. Their diverse perspectives, ranging from internal teams to external partners and customers, offer valuable insights that shape strategic decisions and operational plans.

Whether through providing feedback on product prototypes, advocating for community interests, or allocating resources, stakeholders fuel the momentum of progress.

This collaborative approach not only fosters a sense of ownership and accountability but also cultivates a culture of innovation and adaptability within the organization.

As we build upon the crucial role of stakeholders in organizational change, it's imperative to contemplate the optimal extent of change: is more change preferable, or is less change better?

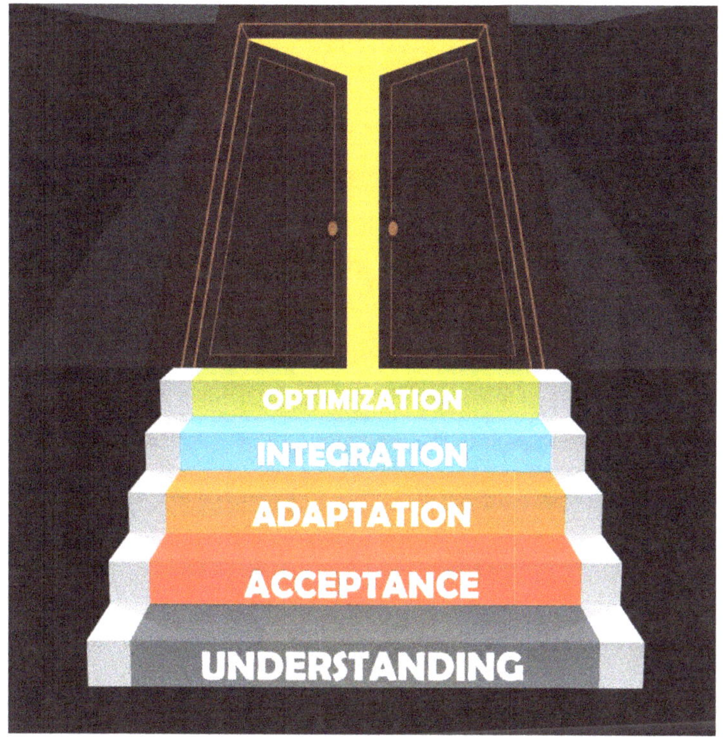

Levels of Change

Different levels of change may lead to pondering which is best. Is more change better, or is less change better? It's a question that often arises when considering organizational transformations. However, since this book is centered on you, the individual within the organization, the approach is straightforward: focus on your own actions and responsibilities.

Various models and philosophies exist, offering four, five, or even six levels of change for organizations to adopt and implement. Regardless of the model or philosophy chosen, what matters most is how effectively you utilize it. The key lies in understanding your role within the chosen framework and executing your part to the best of your ability.

Employees within the organization must also comprehend the model or philosophy the organization employs for change and understand how that model operates. Most importantly, they need to grasp how they fit into the model. Without this, you can begin to break down any positive organizational dynamics and turn down a path of negative organizational dynamics. In essence, leaders of an organization should utilize a change model or philosophy to fulfill their responsibilities effectively—each person owning their part.

Just as organizations are structured in levels or layers, the level of participation for each individual involved in the change process varies. For instance, while the president of the organization bears the ultimate responsibility for ensuring that the change aligns with the company's objectives, your role may or may not directly correspond to your day-to-day responsibilities within the organization. It's entirely plausible that you could assume the role of a lead change agent for a particular aspect of change that extends beyond your typical duties or area of expertise.

Flat or matrix organizations are adept at assigning responsibilities to individuals outside their usual line of responsibility or expertise. Should you find yourself in this position, accept it with enthusiasm and passion because it is an incredible compliment to you and your abilities. Embrace, accept, and excel in these duties and added responsibilities.

In his book *"The 21 Irrefutable Laws of Leadership,"* John Maxwell emphasizes the significance of influence in leadership in the following words:

"Leadership is influence, nothing more, nothing less."

-John C. Maxwell

Maxwell asserts that leadership is fundamentally about influence, highlighting that everyone possesses a level of influence, but not all individuals effectively leverage it to become good leaders. Thus, to enhance one's leadership capacity and impact more people, evaluating the quality of influence is crucial. Maxwell provides practical guidance on gaining influence by valuing people, maintaining integrity, and focusing on personal growth and development.

This leads to the ability to influence others, give them incentives to follow, and inspire respect for your leadership abilities. This influence is very powerful when you are in charge of people outside your normal directorate. Of course, for every positive, there is a negative. In this case, the supervisors of the people assigned to you may feel neglected or interpret the implication as leadership lacking confidence in their ability to lead the change effort.

Countering this is the point made later in this chapter, stating all levels of leadership and supervision must have buy-in to the organizational change, thereby leading the organization to believe all levels of the organization understand the need to assign personnel to someone not in their respective chain of command. Should a supervisor make an issue of this, people should feel confident organizational leadership will resolve the matter.

Your work environment is ever-changing. Things like documents, policies, procedures, IT systems, and production processes are constantly in flux. In this dynamic environment, embracing change that presents significant challenges and promises substantial benefits and rewards is essential for growth and success. Many organizations have policy documents that describe and define how an organization functions. The larger the organization, the more extensive the policy documentation tends to be.

In this regard, Standard Operating Procedures (SOPs) are crucial documents that require frequent updates to align with technological advancements and evolving processes. These SOPs provide clear direction for tasks, ensuring consistency, efficiency, and quality in operations. They are essential for various careers like marketing, cannabis, education, and hospitality. SOPs play a vital role in ensuring regulatory compliance, improving safety, and enabling proper onboarding and training within organizations.[3] They serve as a blueprint for success by systematizing internal processes and promoting a unified approach to operations within an organization.

Moreover, SOPs are a perfect example of organizational documents that undergo frequent changes. As technology, equipment, and processes advance, the relevant SOPs must evolve accordingly. This aligns with the principles of continual improvement process (CIP), a concept often associated with the work of W. Edwards Deming. In the context of CIP, organizations constantly seek ways to enhance efficiency, quality, and effectiveness in their operations. Companies with strong, positive organizational dynamics embrace change as part of their strengths to success.

Processes change not only due to technological advancements but also because even minor improvements contribute to increased product reliability, efficiency, and effectiveness. Each refinement aims to enhance the overall

---

[3]https://www.techtarget.com/searchbusinessanalytics/definition/standard-operating-procedure-SOP

quality and performance of the product or service offered by the organization.[4]

The manufacturing industry is acutely aware of the significance of product reliability, efficiency, and effectiveness. These factors not only contribute to increased profit margins but also provide a competitive advantage in the market. When a process improvement is identified, it becomes imperative to integrate it seamlessly with existing processes to maintain consistency. This integration often involves updating procedural documents that guide employees, even those who work remotely, in adhering to the refined production methods. The ability to seamlessly work in this manner shines a bright light on their organizational dynamics.

Even the smallest changes on the production line can yield significant consumer benefits. That's precisely why companies continuously refine their processes and meticulously document these adjustments in SOPs or similar documents. Without a proactive approach from the organization to enact and integrate these changes, the workforce will run the risk of operating below the organization's desired capacity.

Your actions hold sway over others, reshaping organizational dynamics in the process. How you go about introducing or crafting change can have a profound impact. You might find yourself in the position of spearheading the design or development of the change itself. Essentially, that brilliant idea from someone else or a valuable suggestion from a key customer

---

[4] https://hbr.org/1985/11/implementing-new-technology

now falls under your purview to transform into a concrete plan for adjusting policies, procedures, or techniques.

And guess what? Usually, the individual tasked with this responsibility is regarded as a subject matter expert or possesses the expertise needed to devise the most logical and effective changes required.

In large organizations, the complexity of implementing change necessitates a meticulously developed plan, especially considering the diversity within the workforce, as discussed earlier in this chapter. On the other hand, as a small business owner with just a few employees, you might conceptualize the change plan mentally, perhaps jotting down a few notes to prevent overlooking critical details.

However, regardless of the organization's size, I recommend always committing your plan to paper to ensure nothing is amiss. Also, let others in the organization review and provide input. This will not only support organizational dynamics by including them, but this will also begin the buy-in process.

This approach helps you validate the steps necessary for a successful change.

How To Implement The Change Process?

1 Identify the need for change

2 Define the Change

3 Develop a vision and strategy

5 Implement the Change

4 Communicate the Change

6 Manage resistance

7 Monitor and Evaluate the Change

8 Consolidate and embed the Change

Figure 1: How To Implement The Change Process?
Image Source:
https://change.walkme.com/change-process/

At a minimum, a business owner should document the timeline for implementing change, outlining the steps involved and the milestones for monitoring progress and evaluating the effectiveness of the change. These milestones serve as reference points to validate the proper implementation of the change and measure its impact on various aspects of the business.

In order to create a comprehensive timeline for implementing changes in a business, it is essential to consider key elements such as project start and end dates, key milestones, deadlines, deliverables, task breakdown with dependencies, and estimated completion times.

Utilizing project timeline software with features like Gantt charts can visually represent project schedules and dependencies effectively.[5]

Therein lies the truth.

The late singer, songwriter, and poet Leonard Cohen penned a song titled *"Everybody Knows,"* featuring the lyrics: "Everybody knows that the boat is leaking. Everybody knows that the captain lied." This is reflective of the fact that honesty is paramount for the success of your change effort.

Even if you consider yourself adept at spinning words and evading challenges, attempting to gloss over obstacles in the organization's change implementation is often more time-consuming. It requires more effort to craft elaborate workarounds than simply telling the truth.

Returning to Leonard Cohen's *"Everybody Knows,"* it's evident that while leaders may adeptly sidestep the truth, employees often see through the charade. Despite leaders' attempts to navigate delicate topics with finesse, employees may silently plead for transparency.

I remember organization meetings convened by leadership to discuss the results of a recent organizational climate survey, you

---

[5]https://edrawmind.wondershare.com/timeline/business-timeline-templates.html

know, the one where employees share feedback with leadership. It was clear leadership was grappling with criticism regarding their transparency in communication. When the final topic of the meeting came up, leadership sent up the third most senior figure in the organization, who was highly respected and well-liked, to address this pressing issue.

However, instead of acknowledging a leadership shortfall, they shifted the blame onto the employees, suggesting they simply didn't grasp organizational processes. The room fell into a stunned silence as disbelief spread across the faces of those present. It was a sobering moment, highlighting a glaring leadership deficiency.

It was like a punch to the gut. Witnessing such a blatant leadership shortcoming and then having it brushed off with blame for the staff's understanding shattered employee confidence in leadership.

Many employees had voiced similar concerns in the survey, yet here we were, told that we simply didn't understand. It was disheartening; we were left with expressions of disbelief as if someone were trying to convince us that two plus two equals five.

Additionally, cliques began to develop, and people started sharing common feelings about this. You could hear comments around the water cooler that could put cracks in the current organizational dynamics. You could feel the previously strong dynamics beginning to fracture.

There are two critical aspects to this honesty principle. First, as a leader, it's your responsibility to steer the organization through change and ensure its long-term success, assuming the change is indeed beneficial. Second, it's important to recognize that your team, staff, and employees are more perceptive and capable than you might give them credit for. By providing clear and honest information, you empower them to respond effectively and positively to the challenges ahead.

It also maintains or even strengthens, organizational dynamics because everyone understands the truth. They can discuss the truth as it applies to them or their peers instead of discussing their interpretation of what was told to them.

Imagine you're giving someone directions to a destination. You could say, "You can turn left at the next corner, or if you prefer, you could go up a few blocks and circle back. It's up to you."

However, if you know that turning left at the next corner is the most efficient route, it's better to confidently recommend that option and explain why it's the best choice. Similarly, providing clear guidance and rationale in business and leadership often yields better outcomes than leaving decisions entirely up to others.

Receiving constructive feedback is crucial for success—it fosters buy-in and strengthens organizational dynamics. While the example above may not be perfect, the underlying message remains clear: debating how you communicate with your team is unnecessary.

Some individuals possess the gift of making even dire news sound appealing, but ultimately, nothing surpasses honesty. Securing buy-in from your organization is best achieved through transparent communication.

Pitfalls of Hypocrisy in Organizational Change

Just the other day, I pondered the significant impact of hypocrisy on any change effort. How can one support any endeavor, particularly a change initiative, when leaders or those around them exhibit traits or actions of hypocrisy?

As I contemplated this, a song by the "Beastie Boys" popped into my mind. Yes, the rap rock group from Brooklyn, New York. They had a popular song titled *"Fight for Your Right to Party."* In that song, there's a lyric that goes, "My dad caught me smoking, and he said no way, that hypocrite smokes two packs a day."

This perfectly illustrates the situation where a senior person tries to enforce rules or policies while seen violating them or simply not caring.

If organizational leaders demonstrate behavior contrary to what they're trying to change, how can they expect to successfully implement new rules, policies, procedures, functions, or operations?

It makes you reflect on the negative aspects of organizational dynamics discussed at the beginning of this chapter, doesn't it? It's quite evident that any sign or indication that not everyone, particularly leaders, can't or won't comply or are seen as being forced to accept the change will not only lose credibility but also any motivation for subordinates to take the change seriously.

There's no buy-in here! This can be incredibly destructive to organizational dynamics. I can only imagine how a mid-management or junior person in the organization would react.

Would they think, "Why should I make an effort to implement this change if my superiors are not serious about it?" Some could say, "Do as I say, not as I do."

Although this is a less-than-stellar leadership style, they could get away with it based on the situation. Come on, people, wake up! Change is a team effort manifested by individual desire and attitude.

Notice I did not say anything about skill level. Although it takes skill to make your portion of change effective, it is a given that you have the skill set to do your job; that's why you were hired to the position, right? So, let's go back to the hypocrite. The Merriam-Webster dictionary defines hypocrisy as "behavior that contradicts what one claims to believe or feel."[6]

I know many want to believe hypocrisy is not part of their leadership style, personality, or demeanor. Yes, sure thing; now it's time to check yourself and think critically and honestly over your last few weeks on the job. Point made! Knowing this can impact any change effort, how could it creep into the mix? Better

---

[6] https://www.merriam-webster.com/dictionary/hypocrisy

yet, do you even think about what you are doing to either make the change positive or negative in the eyes of your peers and subordinates?

It won't take much to tear at the basic fiber of any change effort. *What, me, a hypocrite? No way!* Possibly, (more than likely) way! Many of us rarely recognize our hypocrisy or, maybe to a larger extent, refuse to admit our actions are hypocritical. Yes, even you, Mr. CEO, or fast-rising Vice President.

It comes back to you as an individual. It comes down to how your actions are perceived by those around you and those within your sphere of influence. And think of the impact on organizational dynamics. You, at the top, can cripple or positively influence organizational dynamics throughout the organization down to the newest employee. When you see it, call it out. When you are it, be big enough to admit your mistake and don't do it again. When you catch yourself being a hypocrite, and you recognize it, ensure you tell those in your sphere of influence that you recognize what you did and that what you're doing hurts the organizational effort to incorporate the change.

You will witness a higher level of respect for you and will do wonders to keep the team effort strong, just through one individual effort. Good for you and good for the organization!

Observational Opportunities

Observational opportunities become invaluable in identifying areas for change within an organization. Do you find yourself at your desk, pondering better ways to accomplish tasks? Perhaps you participate in a process and see potential for improvement or a different approach. Maybe you've looked at your organization and envisioned ways to conduct business more effectively, efficiently, or even innovatively.

If any of these scenarios resonate with you, what action do you typically take? Merely recognizing an opportunity for change is the first step. Move beyond mere complaints about a process and instead pinpoint actionable improvements to enhance the organization. Whether your idea for change is substantial or minor, understanding the desired end state or the potential impact on the organization is crucial at this initial stage.

Once you've formulated your idea, effective communication becomes imperative. You don't need to be a change management expert, but you should be able to articulate why your proposed vision is valuable for the organization. This ability to communicate the significance of your plan, along with its desired outcomes, is key to gaining support from your supervisor and organizational leadership.

A spark of inspiration can ignite a flame of change within an organization. As you identify opportunities for improvement and devise plans to address them, you embark on a journey of transformation. While investing extra time and effort beyond your regular duties may seem daunting, your dedication speaks volumes about your commitment to the organization. It reflects your inner culture, your values, and your passion for driving positive change.

As your idea gains momentum and evolves into a well-crafted plan, it becomes a beacon of hope and progress. Presenting this plan to organizational leadership showcases your initiative and strategic thinking. It demonstrates your ability to identify challenges and propose effective solutions, earning you respect and recognition within the organization. Better yet, if you communicate to your manager your plan to the point they are comfortable presenting that plan to leadership, you score bonus points across the spectrum of positive traits discussed in this book.

While not every idea may come to fruition, the process of ideation and planning is invaluable. It hones your skills, expands your perspective, and fosters a culture of innovation and continuous improvement. Your willingness to contribute to the organization's success, even outside traditional working hours, sets you apart as a leader and influencer.

As organizational dynamics shift and evolve, your role in driving change becomes increasingly vital. Your efforts ripple through the organization, inspiring others to embrace new ideas and initiatives. With each step forward, you contribute to growth, adaptability, and resilient culture.

To put it plainly, your contributions matter in the dynamic landscape of organizational change. Your ideas, actions, and leadership pave the way for a brighter future. So, embrace the opportunities before you, and together, let us navigate the ever-changing currents of organizational dynamics with purpose, passion, and perseverance.

Chapter 4: Integrity

In this chapter, we'll explore the critical role of integrity in the process of organizational change. We will probe into the significance of integrity at both individual and collective levels, emphasizing its impact on the success and sustainability of change initiatives. By examining the relationship between integrity, buy-in, desire, and individual responsibility, this chapter aims to highlight the importance of maintaining integrity throughout the change process and beyond, ultimately contributing to long-term organizational success.

So, let's begin by delving into the concept of integrity within the context of organizational change. Integrity in the process embodies a quality that hinges on trust in oneself, the organization, and the workforce.

Integrity in an organization refers to the act of behaving honorably, even when unsupervised, and consistently adhering to moral and ethical principles. It involves closing the gap between intentions and actions, ensuring interactions with stakeholders align with ethical standards. Thus, integrity is crucial for building a reputation of reliability, trustworthiness, honesty, and respect within the workplace.

The key aspects of integrity in the workplace include:

1. **Honor and Responsibility:** Taking ownership of decisions and actions.
2. **Ethical Behavior:** Following moral principles even when unobserved.
3. **Consistency:** Acting honestly and transparently at all times.

4. **Reliability:** Being trustworthy in interactions with colleagues and stakeholders.
5. **Respect:** Treating others with dignity and fairness.

Why Organizational Integrity Matters?

First and foremost, integrity forms the bedrock of trust within the organization. Organizations prioritizing integrity benefit from enhanced reputation, customer loyalty, employee retention, and financial performance. Business integrity is not just about compliance but about doing what is right, fostering an ethical culture throughout the organization, and being accountable for mistakes. Organizations need to embed integrity in their DNA by establishing a leadership culture that upholds ethical standards at all levels, and at all times.

When individuals consistently demonstrate honesty, transparency, and ethical behavior, trust naturally flourishes among team members. This trust is essential for effective collaboration, communication, and teamwork. Without it, progress stagnates, and relationships fray, leading to a toxic work environment.

Furthermore, a culture of integrity instills confidence in stakeholders, including clients, investors, and the broader community. When an organization is known for its ethical practices and moral decision-making, it garners respect and loyalty from external parties. This can lead to increased customer satisfaction, stronger investor support, and enhanced brand reputation, all of which are vital for long-term success.

Moreover, integrity serves as a guiding principle during times of change and uncertainty. In today's dynamic business landscape, organizations frequently encounter challenges, whether technological disruptions, market fluctuations, or regulatory changes. In such times, maintaining integrity ensures decisions are made with ethical considerations in mind, safeguarding the organization's reputation and long-term viability.

Finally, a culture of integrity is essential for attracting and retaining top talent. In today's competitive labor market, skilled professionals seek employers who share their values and prioritize ethical conduct. By fostering a reputation for integrity, organizations can attract high-caliber employees who align with the organization's mission and vision, driving innovation and growth.

While it's tempting to assume that every employee possesses a certain level of integrity that will naturally surface during times of change, the reality is more nuanced.

Integrity should not be equated with mere buy-in; it goes beyond that. Individuals take pride in their integrity, and when faced with challenges, they demonstrate the depth of their commitment to maintaining it.

Perhaps even reflecting on your own experiences, you can recall numerous instances where individuals demonstrated or failed to demonstrate integrity. Buy-in to change allows each person's integrity to come into play in a much more significant manner than one might anticipate. Referring back to Chapter 2, it's essential for each employee to introspect and determine if they truly comprehend, believe in, and support the change.

To bolster integrity, leadership must ensure effective communication to deliver a message that accurately articulates the organization's objectives and anticipated outcomes after change implementation. Moreover, the organization must embody the highest standards of integrity; otherwise, integrity becomes irrelevant to the success equation.

Whether the change is substantial, moderate, or minor, integrity remains paramount throughout the process. However, larger changes pose a greater opportunity to test the integrity of both staff and the process.

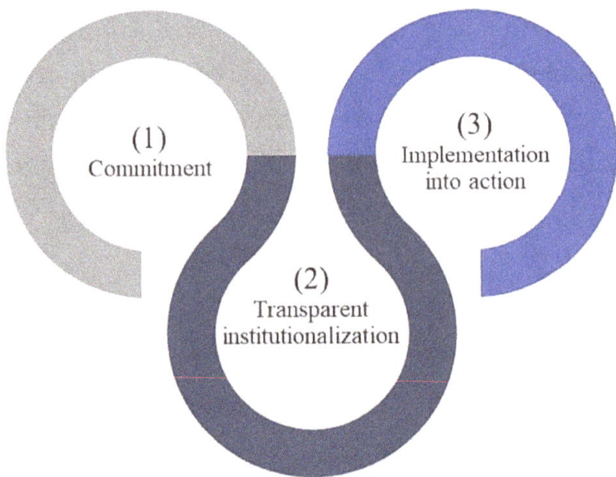

Figure 2: Integrity Meter Diagram
Image Source:
https://onlinelibrary.wiley.com/doi/full/10.1111/basr.12329

Integrity in Change: Your Role and Approach

Do you have the desire to improve? First of all, remember that your desire isn't about whether you enjoy it or not. It's not about being a knight in shining armor to the process but rather about recognizing that your contribution to the organization can enhance the change process through your efforts to improve it.

Good leaders will get the job done, regardless! Smart leaders will accomplish the same task without causing collateral damage. Note that there's a distinct difference between the two. Which type of leader would you prefer? A leader who focuses solely on achieving the end goal, often disregarding the efforts of their team and the available resources, will likely encounter negative outcomes during the change process. This approach can lead to dissatisfaction in the workforce. Leadership and management expert Peter Drucker states:

"Never push loyal people to the point where they don't give a damn."

Conversely, a leader who considers the needs of their people, the available resources, and the demands of the organization and recognizes risks such as burnout and exhaustion when pushing forward embodies a more effective leadership style. While the latter leadership style is preferable, the reality is that dealing with senior leaders who adopt the first approach may be inevitable. Nonetheless, your efforts will still contribute to the ongoing change process and make a difference.

Various factors, including leadership, the work environment, and organizational priorities, influence your level of desire. In Chapter 6, we'll explore how distractions, often referred to as "shiny objects," can disrupt organizational focus. Despite external influences, the intangible trait of striving to do your best remains significant. You have the power to control your desire for excellence, but external forces can sway your motivation, causing fluctuations in effort and productivity as you work towards achieving your goals.

A perspective to consider regarding your integrity in supporting change is to adopt a single philosophy: you are an integral part of the organization, thus making you inherently part of the change solution. However, it's crucial to emphasize that organizational buy-in from the workforce is essential for this philosophy to succeed. How you approach the new and improved process reflects your commitment as a member of the organization.

As discussed in Chapter 3, understanding and fulfilling your role to the best of your ability is paramount. Anything less risks undercutting the organization and undermining the change process at your level.

Indeed, it's true that even at the most junior levels of the organization, you can undermine a change process. Depending on how crucial your individual skill set is to the change, you might wield more influence over the process. However, it's vital not to exploit this influence as a bargaining chip. Remember, integrity is at stake here. Consider yourself as a user of the change process, you hope those involved acted with responsibility to contribute positively and uphold the integrity of the initiative.

Consider, for instance, a change process involving a software function you simply dislike or believe to be flawed. In such a scenario, you might be inclined to revert to the old way of doing things, undermining the intended change process, and negatively impacting any follow-on steps, including the follow-up process designed to embed the change in the daily norm. Even worse, you might attempt to incorporate the step according to your preferences, thereby completely undermining the rationale and effort invested in the change.

The appropriate course of action is to provide feedback on how the process affects you. If your feedback is valid, your supervisor will acknowledge it and take steps to adjust the process accordingly. However, if your assessment is incorrect or the prescribed action is necessary due to other considerations, you will have to comply. In this situation, your integrity is tested—whether your faith in the feedback system pays off.

You Are a Part of the Organization

Ask yourself: Do you adhere to the prescribed orderliness as a team member, or do you ultimately decide to leave for another job because you no longer feel satisfied or part of the team? It may sound harsh, but it's a reality many face. How many people do you know who left an organization because they felt their input wasn't valued or because they had issues with their supervisors or the organization's direction? If this is you, return to the philosophy that emphasizes integrity, and remember you are part of the solution. Your commitment to fulfilling your role to the best of your ability is crucial.

In fact, integrity at all levels is crucial for the success of any change initiative. We will delve further into it in Chapter 6, "In it for the Long Haul," your ongoing commitment to the desired end state of change will determine the long-term success of institutionalizing change within your organization. Your integrity, demonstrated throughout the change implementation process, doesn't end once the project is complete. It requires integrity to address deviations from the specifics of the overall change initiative, whether by peers, seniors, or subordinates. An intangible reward from the change process comes when, at a time in the future, you explain the process to new employees as if it has always been this way.

So, reflecting on each phase of the change plan should serve as motivation to take action when you observe incidents that could jeopardize the success of the change initiative—not to mention the significant effort invested in the project to that point.

Bear in mind that integrity is not just a buzzword; it's a fundamental pillar that underpins the success of organizational change. From fostering trust and collaboration to enhancing the organization's reputation and attracting top talent, the benefits of integrity are far-reaching. It serves as a guiding principle during times of uncertainty and ensures that decisions are made with ethical considerations in mind.

Moreover, integrity is essential for maintaining momentum and motivation throughout the change process as you drive toward the desired end state. By adding integrity to our actions and decisions, we not only contribute to the success of change initiatives but also cultivate a culture of trust, respect, and accountability within our organization.

Chapter 5: Train of Change

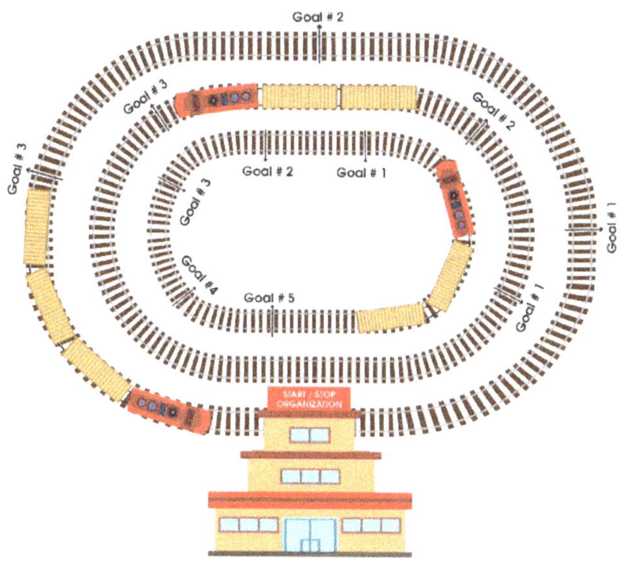

Now that we have discussed the significance of integrity, in this chapter, we will begin a stimulating journey through the diverse landscape of organizational transformation. As American author H. Jackson Brown Jr. once wisely said:

"The best preparation for tomorrow is doing your best today."

Just as each day presents an opportunity to lay the groundwork for future success, every aspect of organizational change holds the potential to shape the trajectory of the enterprise in profound ways. By embracing the ethos of perpetual evolution and relentless pursuit of excellence, we set the stage for transformative shifts that propel our organizations toward a brighter, more resilient future.

Throughout this chapter, we'll look at the ways to manage change with energy and determination. We'll understand that every choice we make, every action we take, and every time we work hard helps our organization improve. We'll take inspiration from intelligent people who came before us and from what we've learned in real life. So, get on board the train of change, where you're not just in for the ride but the one steering the course of transformation in your organization.

Imagine this journey like a train with many cars trailing behind, each representing a different part of your organization. Just as it takes time for a train to pick up speed and zoom down the tracks with all its cargo, starting change in your organization needs a slow and steady approach. Begin slowly, let the engines of change do their job, and gradually pick up speed as you move forward.

As the one in charge, you, or you and your team, have a big role to play in making this happen. Think of it like loading a train with cargo—it's best to be careful and steady to keep everything on track. Once you start moving, you'll see the change taking hold in the organization as you move in the right direction.

Think of each train as a team. As a team member, you have a role in the success of what this change represents. Success on this train includes constructive meetings, beneficial briefings, unity of tasks within the change plan, or just a successful day at your organization. No one person is more important than the next person. Think of an experience you had checking in to a nice hotel. Someone greets you in the lobby, and then another greeting at the check-in desk. The bellhop handling your bags offers a cheery hello, and all the other services offered will greet you equally well. Each one is designed to make you feel comfortable during your stay to ensure you will experience a memorable stay at their hotel. This would best emulate the atmosphere you would expect to see on the train of change.

Your individual performance day in and day out makes the organization who it is and makes it the ultimate success. Working with others in a productive manner on the train of change is a conduit to this successful team. This is really about each one of us and our minute-by-minute, hour-by-hour, day-by-day positive contribution to our tiny little piece of the bigger pie.

When it's time for the next significant change, you need to figure out what parts of the organization need to be on board. As the train leaves the station, representing the start of the change, it's important to explain what the change is all about, how it will happen, and what we're aiming for in the end. At each stop or goal that's depicted in the illustration, we handle what needs to be done, making necessary adjustments before moving forward toward our destination.

Considering your organization's leadership has already hashed out the details of the next change, including its purpose, benefits for the organization, and the desired outcome, you can fill in appropriate details to the plan. This planning phase may coincide with ongoing change efforts or recently completed plans that are now in the follow-up phase.

Let's take, for instance, a significant administrative change that directly impacts the quality of life for employees. Once this change is fully implemented, its effects may not be immediately apparent. Instead, they might unfold gradually over time, revealing themselves through various iterations and adjustments within the organization.

Staying with the example above, a new company policy will alter how to accrue and use vacation time. Most employees won't feel the full impact of this change until they take time off under the new policy for the first time. As this adjustment period plays out, the train of change keeps chugging along, albeit at a slower pace initially, gradually gaining momentum as the organization adapts to the new way of doing things.

You can sense the energy of change. Change causing an adrenaline rush? That's surprising! Usually, change brings headaches and anxiety. Ask yourself, have I ever felt excited about change, whether in the organization, my work area, or my life? Well, perhaps if the change aligns with my preferences or if it's something I'm familiar with. Could it be that I'm highly motivated to engage with the change? Maybe more often than not, I'm probably not thrilled about what's coming. Why is that?

Let's explore the potential reasons or influences that could genuinely spark excitement and enthusiasm among the organization, specific individuals, or the entire workforce. Once all personnel board the train of change, you should have nothing but excitement and enthusiasm all around you. As mentioned before, you may get an adrenaline rush that could stem from understanding the benefits, vision, or purpose behind the upcoming change. Wouldn't it be wonderful if you could announce a change to the workforce, and every employee, including leadership, instantly comprehended and valued what you're proposing?

Well, I regret to inform you that such a scenario is highly unlikely. Even with some explanation, simply announcing a change won't likely yield positive progress. Instead, you may encounter the opposite reaction – a lack of enthusiasm or engagement with your announcement. You might even witness a sense of apathy, with employees showing little interest or motivation. On the other hand, there could be an adrenaline rush, but not the kind you hope for – rather, it might prompt employees to head for the exits!

We spoke of buy-in in Chapter 1, and to align buy-in with the train of change, we learned how important buy-in is to any change project. When announcing an upcoming change, the manager must ensure they are ready with as many facts as possible and prepared to answer questions with something more than "I don't know" or "I'll get back to you."

When considering a plan the organization intends to execute or implement, what aspect are you more concerned with – the broader, overarching vision or the nitty-gritty details that outline specific steps and the approach to implementing change? Hopefully, your focus leans towards the latter—the micro details that provide a clear roadmap for change implementation.

Yeah, I get it. Reading through all those details might seem like a chore. After all, who has the time or patience for that? But trust me, diving into the nitty-gritty of the plan is where the real excitement lies. It may sound boring at first, but once you start delving into the specifics, you'll realize just how crucial each step is for driving the organization forward.

Understanding your role within the grand scheme of things is key to feeling truly invested in the change process. When you see how your efforts fit into the bigger picture and how they impact other areas of the organization, it's incredibly empowering. It's like connecting the dots and realizing that you're part of something much larger than yourself. And let me tell you, that feeling of inclusion and teamwork is nothing short of exhilarating.

Imagine passing the baton to the next phase of the change plan, knowing that you've played a significant role in laying the groundwork for success. That adrenaline rush you feel isn't just about the thrill of the moment—it's a testament to the time and effort you've invested in making the change happen. And the level of buy-in you'll have? It'll be off the charts, fueled by your dedication and commitment every step of the way.

Let's look at the stress of change for a moment. You'd think that someone who thrives on stress—let's call them a "stress junky" – would be the perfect candidate to embrace organizational change with open arms. After all, they're used to pushing their limits, taking on new challenges, and making a real impact in the organization. Having a stress junky on your change team sounds like a dream come true, right?

You'd expect them to dive headfirst into any opportunity for growth and innovation, eager to contribute their unique perspective and drive the change forward. And in many ways, having a stress junky on board can be an advantage. You can count on them to be fully committed and put in the time and effort needed to see the change plan through to the end.

Consider a different scenario: what if your supervisor is the stress junky? Suddenly, the whole approach to change takes on a new dimension. Pushy leaders who thrive on stress may have a lower tolerance for delays or deviations from the plan. They might prioritize the change process to such an extent that it disrupts your usual workflow, causing you to fall behind on your regular tasks. While it may be difficult to imagine supervisors acting this way, the impact of the change on your department or the company overall could influence how the stress junky responds.

What about the lack of excitement surrounding change? When an organization initiates a change plan, there's often a surge of excitement and adrenaline. However, not everyone approaches the execution of a change plan with fairness or a genuine commitment to embracing the change's intent. When the change process begins positively and gains momentum, the organization can make significant progress in a short period. However, amidst this positive energy and momentum, negative forces may be at play to hinder the intended change's progress.

Some of the pitfalls include poor decision-making. By poor decisions, I mean instances where individuals disregard honesty, integrity, or a logical approach to executing the change. Examples of this inappropriate behavior could include overstepping authorized boundaries. You might observe situations where an individual in charge of one area arbitrarily assigns tasks to someone without the authority to perform them. In such cases, confusion, disorganization, and frustration quickly emerge among managers and peers. This erodes trust among managers and peers, leading to tension, discord, and a significant distraction from the organization's ultimate goals.

You should think of your train of change as a tight network of people and teams. You don't have the liberty of a team bonded together primarily because they are confined inside one of the train cars. However, if the team is strong and acting like they are on one of the train cars, you'll see less disruption as the change plan moves from goal to goal.

In an organization where a significant portion of the workforce is mobile due to the nature of the business or organizational policy, the dynamics are quite different from those in a traditional office environment where employees are typically situated near their managers. In such mobile-centric organizations, managers themselves may also be on the move while performing their duties. Consequently, a manager might be more inclined to delegate tasks to an employee or subordinate who happens to be nearby, even if their decision may serve the manager's immediate needs but could be counterproductive to the overall change effort.

This scenario becomes counterproductive because the employee is likely working within an area that aligns with the overarching change vision, and their tasks are probably following the directives provided to their manager. While it's not to suggest that managers wouldn't overstep their boundaries in a more controlled environment, it's more plausible that a closer working environment could facilitate better oversight. Nonetheless, the possibility remains that a manager might overstep boundaries, leading to confusion and frustration among the workforce.

This situation underscores the importance of exerting control over the initial steps and actions taken by the workforce when the change plan begins or when the train leaves the station. Leadership, demonstrating a commitment to change, should also exhibit a commitment to its execution from day one. It's not about micromanagement but rather a proactive and intelligent approach to ensuring the successful implementation of change. Senior leaders should provide additional oversight and allocate time to ensure the initial actions necessary for executing the change plan are carried out effectively.

Such involvement is not micromanagement; it's a strategic effort to ensure the team members pay the appropriate level of attention to the initial stages of the change effort. You remember that timeframe when the train slowly leaves the station. This is actually the best time to expect a higher level of involvement, as it is crucial to lay a solid foundation to ensure no one waivers from the initial steps. Subordinate managers should expect and welcome this level of involvement, recognizing its significance in achieving successful change outcomes.

The next question you would want to ask yourself, which also applies to managers, is how the organization can allow this type of behavior in the change process. Well, suppose you look at it from the perspective of senior management in a large organization. In that case, those leaders often have a lot on their plates, and some of the specifics delegated to lower management levels may not come to their attention for some time, if at all. From the managers' perspective, there's a desire, whether it's beneficial or not, to execute the change in a manner they believe is best, within the confines of the change plan, for the organization.

What's puzzling about this is these same managers, in all likelihood, work together daily and do not witness or experience errant behavior or action. It's not a typical characteristic of organizational norms. From a realistic standpoint, many managers, as peers, are quite competitive. This competitiveness brings both advantages and challenges. Don't be misled; it's indeed a fact of life in the workplace. Setting that aside, let's consider one possible reason why this behavior may persist.

The impact of change on individuals is profound. Change often follows significant events, whether natural disasters like earthquakes, man-made incidents such as active shooter situations, or personal tragedies like death, divorce, or family crises. Even smaller events, such as a fire in the building that didn't directly affect you or your company, can still lead to noticeable changes in people. If an event causes the train of change to slow down or stop, it must be done so in a thoughtful way to ensure the momentum you have takes the burden to hopefully reduce as much stress as possible.

Let's focus on a scenario most of us are familiar with- personal tragedy. When such an event strikes, it affects you directly. Unlike a colleague at the desk next to you or a supervisor down the hall, this event is internal to you, and that's what makes all the difference. Personal tragedies have a deep impact, altering how you approach your job and interact with others and how you respond to various work-related situations.

Some events prompt introspection and lead you to reconsider your approach to various aspects of life. Conversely, other events may dampen your enthusiasm or cause you to prioritize differently, leading to a shift in your behavior and attitude. You may want to get off the train of change because, at this point, you don't want to do anything more than the minimums in your job and nothing else. Whether or not you're aware of it, those around you often notice these changes. Comments like, "You seem preoccupied lately," or "You've been acting differently," serve as indications that the event has had a visible impact on you.

Similarly, major natural disasters occurring in your vicinity can be a catalyst for significant changes. Consider the aftermath of hurricanes like Katrina or Sandy, which compel businesses of all sizes to adapt and revise their operations until a new sense of normalcy is established.

All these examples tie back to the metaphor of the train of change. Just like a train, change starts gradually, gains momentum, and operates smoothly between stops. At each stop or goal, there's an opportunity to reassess, replenish, and prepare for the next phase or goal before gradually moving forward again. Recognizing and respecting this continuous cycle is essential for the success of any change initiative.

Chapter 6: In It For The Long Haul

In our final chapter, we will delve into the concept of being "In It For The Long Haul." We will explore the importance of commitment and perseverance in organizational change efforts, emphasizing the significance of believing in the value of each change initiative and recognizing its potential impact over the long term.

Additionally, we will discuss the enduring nature of organizational policies and processes and how leadership shapes organizational evolution. We will also address the challenges posed by distractions, known as "shiny objects," and provide insights into effectively managing them within the context of change implementation.

So, let's begin by understanding what it means to be "in it for the long haul?" It means having the conviction to believe in the value of each change initiative and recognizing its impact over the long term. Even if your tenure within the organization is not defined, organizational policies and processes are intended to endure, shaping the culture and norms over time. While technological advancements may prompt updates, certain policies have stood the test of time, becoming ingrained in the fabric of the organization.

Efforts invested in implementing changes that will benefit the organization for years to come are truly exhilarating. If you had the opportunity to return to a former company years later, you could witness firsthand how some changes have flourished while others have faltered. Conversations with long-term employees shed light on the reasons behind the persistence, adaptation, or abandonment of specific policies. Often, leadership changes usher in policy shifts, highlighting the dynamic nature of organizational evolution.

Imagine returning to the organization where you once worked and encountering a former colleague who, during your previous tenure, expressed skepticism about a particular change initiative. However, you now see this individual occupying a senior position within the company. You think that over the long tenure of this person, their performance overcame any obstructive behavior they exhibited for that particular change process. Unless you hear a first-hand account of whether this person continued not to favor this change, you must assume they supported organizational change in the aggregate. It becomes evident when given the opportunity, power, or influence to effect change, people readily embrace it.

You've likely encountered individuals who seize any chance to reverse or modify past policy changes. Whether or not those changes remain part of the company's current practices is beside the point. What truly matters is the attitude of these former colleagues. Are they actively contributing to solutions or perpetuating problems within the organization? Sustaining any change is very hard unless the organizational norms align with it. If your organizational norm is to complete a project, put it behind you, and then move on to the next project, you will never sustain a change. All the work you do will go to waste unless you can validate the effectiveness of the change over time.

As stated before, once the change becomes part of the daily norm, it is equally hard to reverse or modify it. Bringing you back into the conversation, why would you put forth the effort to embrace an organizational change just to see it go away?

Are you familiar with shiny objects? In their literal sense, they typically adorn shelves, catching the eye with their smooth, glossy surfaces. However, the term takes on a metaphorical meaning in a workplace setting. It refers to distractions that captivate individuals in positions of influence within the organization, causing them to veer off course from the change process.

Something someone feels is important or a discovery they've made along the way that they feel deserves attention is a working-level definition of a shiny object. To the senior members of the organization: Don't allow shiny objects to divert your focus from the overall goal of organizational change. While something important to someone (senior) does merit consideration, it cannot override the plan. A manager of change should anticipate events that may impact the change process. Change agents must be adept at placing shiny objects appropriately on the shelf. This means addressing the person or persons who use shiny objects to derail the train of change. Moving forward, you can ensure that the focus remains on the process the organization agreed to.

Occasionally, a shiny object may demand immediate attention if it affects completing the current step in the change implementation process. In such cases, allocate the necessary attention and respond decisively. If the shiny object starts causing significant unintended impacts, such as requiring additional or expensive resources, senior management should review the situation and anticipate any potential issues in the remaining steps of the process. Simultaneously, managers should analyze lessons learned from past change processes to carefully assess potential impacts. The easy answer is to stick to the plan.

Smaller issues resulting from shiny objects can be a positive aspect of the process. These adjustments indicate that personnel involved in the change understand the significance and implications for their department or the organization as a whole. Managers should acknowledge these details and express appreciation to the individuals for their attention to detail.

How can you determine if the change implementation is effective? Well, first and foremost, consider your overall sentiment toward the change. Reflect on your role in the change process and gauge the organization's collective attitude toward the change. Depending on the scale of the change, subtle reactions may not be immediately noticeable.

Ideally, you should feel positive about your contribution to the change process and observe signs of organizational growth as a result. A clear indicator of success is when long-term employees share anecdotes about how things were done previously with newer colleagues. Although this realization may take some time to emerge, hearing comparisons between "then" and "now" is rewarding.

Pay close attention to the tone of these comments. If employees express relief at no longer adhering to outdated practices and describe the old way of doing things as archaic, it signifies a victory for the change initiative.

Remember, relevance is key. If a change isn't relevant to you, why bother paying attention? Because the change will improve the company at large as it improves those involved in the change process. The relevance to you should be that if it's good for them, it's good for me. Hopefully, the change process relevant to you will yield similar feelings from those not impacted. It's crucial to establish relevance both in the present and in the future. Institutional changes often occur when there's a shift at the highest levels of the organization. Leaders reach senior positions for a reason—usually due to their proven track record and ability to manage effectively.

I've observed interviews with new CEOs expressing their commitment to maintaining the company's positive momentum while making necessary adjustments to remain competitive. This embodies the concept of keeping it relevant. Sometimes, a leadership change is made to "right the ship" in response to a decline in market share, influence, or innovation. This will bring about numerous changes to get the company back on track and return to a positive organizational norm previously held.

As an employee, such changes signal potential shifts in the organization's direction and operations. While they underscore the relevance of the changes, they also highlight the potential challenges and disruptions they may bring. Ultimately, these organizational changes impact the entire organization, influencing its bottom line, the ability to meet consumer demands, and overall well-being. Are you still in it for the long haul? I hope so; we need you.

Relevant changes are essential for maintaining organizational competitiveness and ensuring long-term sustainability. Among these changes are improvements to the quality of life for the workforce. The range of quality-of-life programs is extensive and could include initiatives such as childcare facilities or support programs, collaborative floor plans that encourage employee interaction, and workplace aesthetics designed to enhance productivity.

Changes that align with the organization's culture can be all that some employees need to support a change effort.

Does change ever stop? No, it doesn't! Think about how many clothing style changes you've gone through in your lifetime. How many different hairstyles have you tried? You've likely experienced different companies and held multiple positions within a company. Each of these involves change, albeit of a different type.

Organizational change differs from personal change in that you have less control over organizational change. However, the areas of control you do have in the change process are significant. Don't underestimate your significance in the change process or think that your role isn't valuable to the company.

Even something as simple as showing up on time for change-related meetings and being prepared contributes to the overall success of the change process.

Respected keynote speaker and leadership expert Molly Fletcher lists ten things that require zero talent. Each, when adhered to in good faith, gives you an opportunity to be that person the organization needs. Here are the ten things that require zero talent:

1. Being on time
2. Work ethic
3. Effort
4. Body language
5. Fnergy
6. Attitude
7. Passion
8. Being coachable
9. Doing extra
10. Being prepared

Consider the opposite scenario: late to or not attending the meeting or not prepared. How does that benefit the efforts of your peers? It's disrespectful and unprofessional. It's essential to emphasize the importance of your role in the change process.

Change is constant in life, so the sooner you accept that, the less impact it will have on your personal and professional life.

The ultimate question is: does, will, or can the change make a difference in the end? The answer lies in the determined end state and how effectively you implement the change.

The effectiveness of change hinges on how the team executes it. While this may sound simple, as discussed in this book, change is only as difficult as the team or organization makes it—how difficult they choose to make it.

All in all, staying committed for the long term is crucial for organizational change success. We've learned it's vital to believe in the value and enduring potential of each change. We also discussed how policies shape an organization over time and the challenge of staying focused amidst distractions.

It's important to address shiny objects while keeping our eyes on the main goal. Making change relevant and aligning it with our culture is vital for success. Remember, every small action matters in the journey of change. Ultimately, success depends on everyone's effort and dedication, but it comes down to you and your attitude to contribute to that success.

You, yes you, can change your organization through a proactive, positive approach to any change initiative. You can make a difference. You can influence co-workers, organizations, partner companies, and change efforts by being that person in the room who others see as an asset to the team, a go-to person.

You, you, you. Be the one!